Quiz 4.

MW01235791

Reading American History

The Dutch in New Amsterdam

Written by Melinda Lilly
Illustrated by Laura Jacobsen

Educational Consultants
Kimberly Weiner, Ed.D
Betty Carter, Ed.D

Rourke
Publishing LLC
Vero Beach, Florida 32963

© 2003 Rourke Publishing LLC

All rights reserved. No part of this book may be reproduced or utilized in any form or by any means, electronic, or mechanical including photocopying, recording, or by any information storage and retrieval system without permission in writing from the publisher.

www.rourkepublishing.com

For Mom and Dad, with gratitude for a lifetime of love and encouragement
—L. J.

Designer: Elizabeth J. Bender

Library of Congress Cataloging-in-Publication Data

Lilly, Melinda.
   The Dutch in New Amsterdam / Melinda Lilly; illustrated by Laura Jacobsen.
      p. cm. — (Reading American history)
   Summary: A simple introduction to the history of New Amsterdam, from its establishment by the Dutch until its conquest by the English in 1664.
   ISBN 1-58952-367-9
   1. Dutch Americans—New York (State)—New York—History—Juvenile literature. 2. Stuyvesant, Peter, 1592-1672—Juvenile literature. 3. New York (N.Y.)—History—Colonial period, ca. 1600-1775—Juvenile literature. [1. New York (N.Y.)—History—Colonial period, ca. 1600-1775. 2. Dutch Americans. 3. Stuyvesant, Peter, 1592-1672.] I. Jacobsen, illus. II. Title.

F128.4 .L55 2002
974.7'10043931—dc21   2002017043

Cover Illustration: Peter Stuyvesant stands at the New Amsterdam wall.

Printed in the USA

Time Line

Help students follow this story by introducing important events in the Time Line.

1609   Henry Hudson explores the Hudson River.

1614   Dutch fur traders in Fort Nassau (south of what is now Albany, New York)

1626   Dutch buy Manhattan from Native Americans for $24 worth of goods.

1626   Fort Amsterdam built in New Amsterdam.

1664   New Amsterdam becomes English and is renamed New York.

1673   The Dutch retake New York and rename it New Orange.

1674   New Orange becomes English again and is called New York.

Many Dutch people left Holland and came to America. They hoped to make money.

Getting off the ship in America

The Dutch bought furs from the **Native Americans**.

Buying fur

The Dutch shipped the furs to Holland. There, the furs sold for a high price.

The ship to Holland

In 1626, the Dutch bought the **island** of **Manhattan**. The Dutch paid the Native Americans with **trinkets** worth about 24 dollars. It was a low price.

Buying Manhattan

The Dutch built the town of **New Amsterdam** on the island. In 1664, English ships of war came to town.

Ships near the New Amsterdam fort

"Give up or we will attack," the English said.

Getting the cannon ready to fire

The people wanted peace. They asked the **governor** to give up.

Talking it over with Governor **Peter Stuyvesant**

The Dutch gave up without a fight. New Amsterdam became English.

The governor signs the peace deal.

It also got a new name. . . . New Amsterdam is now called New York City.

Looking at New York City, today

Word List

governor (GUV ur nur)—The head of government for a state or other area

island (EYE lund)—Land that is surrounded by water and is too small to be a continent

Manhattan (man HAT n)—An island in New York City

Native Americans (NAY tiv uh MER ih kunz)—Members of the peoples native to North America; American Indians

New Amsterdam (NOO AM ster dam)—The Dutch town that became New York City

Stuyvesant, Peter (STY vuh sunt, PEA tur)—A Dutch governor, Peter Stuyvesant surrendered New Amsterdam to the English.

trinkets (TRING kits)—Items of little worth, often small

Books to Read

Banks, Joan, and Arthur M. Schlesinger. *Peter Stuyvesant: Dutch Military Leader*. Chelsea House, 2000.

Kalman, Bobbie. *Life in a Longhouse Village*. Crabtree Publishing, 2001.

Krizner, L. J., and Lisa Sita. *Peter Stuyvesant: New Amsterdam and the Origins of New York*. Powerkids, 2002.

Stefoff, Rebecca. *The Colonies*. Marshall Cavendish Corporation, 2000.

Websites to Visit

www.geocities.com/Athens/Styx/6497/newnether.html

www.hudsonvalley.org/web/phil-slav.html

www.lihistory.com/vault/hs305b1v.htm

www.coins.nd.edu/ColCoin/ColCoinIntros/Wampum.intro.html

www.nnp.org/project/timeline.html

Index